AF227650

PUFFIN

Amazing Facts About Nature's Colorful Seabirds for Kids

Dylanna Press

ISBN: 9781647904357 (pb); 9781647904685 (hc)
Publisher: Dylanna Publishing, Inc.
First Edition: 2025

10 9 8 7 6 5 4 3 2 1

For information about special discounts for bulk purchases, please contact:
orders@dylannapublishing.com
Dylanna Publishing, Inc.
www.dylannapublishing.com

Contents

Fun Fact: Puffins are the official bird of Newfoundland and Labrador.

Meet the Puffin

SPLASH! A small black and white bird pops up from beneath the waves, its beak stuffed with silvery fish arranged like a colorful mustache. Meet the Atlantic puffin—one of the most beloved and instantly recognizable seabirds in the world!

Puffins are extraordinary ocean birds. They spend most of their lives at sea, gliding over the chilly waters of the North Atlantic and diving deep below the surface to hunt. You can find them from the coasts of Maine and eastern Canada all the way to Iceland, Norway, and the rocky cliffs of the British Isles.

The Atlantic puffin (*Fratercula arctica*) is the best known of the three puffin species. The other two are the

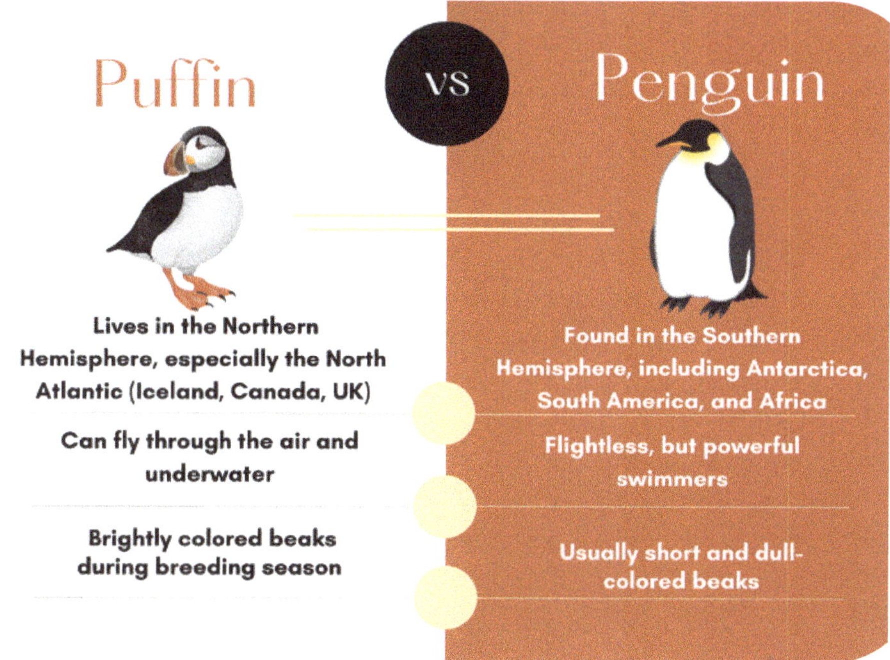

horned puffin and tufted puffin, which live in the North Pacific. All puffins belong to the Alcidae family, which also includes auks, murres, and guillemots and are built for both flying through the air and swimming underwater.

What makes puffins so special? They're speedy underwater hunters, devoted cliffside parents, and incredible long-distance travelers. They can dive over 60 meters deep, flap their wings up to 400 times per minute, and journey thousands of miles across the open ocean without any landmarks.

Puffins are sometimes called "clowns of the sea" or "sea parrots" because of their bright beaks and silly expressions. But there's nothing funny about their survival skills—these tough little birds can withstand fierce ocean storms, dive to incredible depths, and raise their young on some of the most challenging coastlines in the world.

Once hunted for food and feathers, puffins have made a big comeback thanks to conservation efforts. Today, millions of these colorful seabirds still follow their ancient paths—diving, nesting, and thriving along the wild edges of the world.

What Do Puffins Look Like?

Atlantic puffins are small, stocky seabirds built for life both in the air and underwater. Adults grow to about 10 to 12 inches (25 to 30 cm) long with a wingspan of 20 to 24 inches (51 to 61 cm). They weigh between 14 to 18 ounces (400 to 500 grams)—roughly the weight of a can of soup!

The most striking feature of a breeding puffin is its large, colorful beak. During mating season, the beak becomes a brilliant display of orange, red, yellow, and sometimes blue. This oversized beak, called a bill, can grow up to 2 inches (5 cm) long and is perfectly shaped for catching and holding multiple small fish at once.

Puffins have bold black-and-white feathers, or plumage, that make them easy to spot. Their backs, wings, and heads are deep black, while their chests and bellies are bright white. During breeding season, their faces turn pale with white facial discs, making their colorful beaks and bright orange eyes stand out even more.

Their legs and webbed feet also turn a striking orange in spring and summer. These strong, webbed feet help them swim underwater and provide excellent grip on the rocky cliff faces where they nest.

After breeding season, puffins go through a dramatic change. They molt—shedding their colorful beak plates and facial feathers—and take on a duller look for winter. Their smaller gray beaks and darker faces help them blend in with the gray ocean waters where they spend most of their lives.

Puffins' short wings and compact, torpedo-shaped bodies make them excellent swimmers, using their wings like flippers. But flying isn't easy! To stay airborne, puffins beat their wings rapidly, up to 400 times per minute, reaching speeds of 55 miles per hour (88 km/h).

Fun Fact: A puffin's beak is not solid but hollow inside, which keeps it lightweight even though it looks huge.

Fun Fact: Atlantic puffins are the only puffin species that live in the Atlantic Ocean.

Where Do Puffins Live?

Atlantic puffins are true citizens of the North Atlantic Ocean. These hardy seabirds live in the cold, nutrient-rich waters that circle the northern parts of both the Atlantic and Arctic oceans. You can find them from the coasts of Maine and eastern Canada, north to Greenland, and across to Iceland, the Faroe Islands, Norway, and the British Isles.

During most of the year—about eight to nine months—puffins live entirely at sea. They float, dive, and fly across vast stretches of open ocean, following fish riding the currents. The water is often just above freezing, but puffins are built for life in this harsh, chilly world.

When breeding season begins in late spring, puffins return to land to nest on coastal cliffs and offshore islands. They prefer steep, grassy areas where they can dig burrows in the soft ground. These nesting areas, called colonies, can be huge— some are home to hundreds of thousands of birds!

The largest puffin colonies in the world are in Iceland, which hosts about 60 percent of the global Atlantic puffin population. Other big colonies can be found in Scotland, Norway, and the Faroe Islands. In North America, puffins nest in places like Newfoundland and Eastern Egg Rock off the coast of Maine.

Puffins are picky about where they nest. The best sites have soft but stable soil for digging, access to rich fishing waters, and steep cliffs that help them take off quickly. Most importantly, they must be safe from land predators like foxes and rats.

But puffin homes are under threat. Climate change is warming the oceans, changing fish patterns, and making it harder for puffins to find enough food. Some old nesting sites are no longer ideal as sea levels rise and weather patterns shift.

Super Swimmers – Puffin Adaptations

Puffins are built for a life that's part bird, part fish! From sky to sea, every part of their body is adapted to help them survive in the cold, wild waters of the North Atlantic.

- **Underwater Flying:** Puffins are expert underwater swimmers. They use their wings like flippers to "fly" through the water, diving as deep as 200 feet (60 meters) to chase fish. Their compact bodies and dense bones help them dive fast and turn quickly.

- **Waterproof Feathers:** Puffins have two layers of feathers: a dense, fluffy undercoat that traps warm air, and waterproof outer feathers that keep them dry. They spend hours each day preening, spreading oil from a special gland to keep their feathers waterproof and in perfect condition.

- **Specialized Beak:** That famous colorful beak isn't just for show! During breeding season, it develops backward-pointing spines on the roof and tongue that help puffins hold multiple slippery fish crosswise in their mouths. They can carry up to 30 small fish at once back to their chicks.

- **Powerful Wings:** While puffins may look clumsy in flight, their short, powerful wings can beat up to 400 times per minute. This rapid wing-beat allows them to fly at speeds up to 55 mph (88 km/h) and switch smoothly between air and water.

- **Exceptional Vision:** Puffins have excellent eyesight both above and below water. Special muscles can change the shape of their eye lenses, helping them focus clearly whether they're spotting fish from the air or chasing them underwater.

- **Salt Removal:** Like other seabirds, puffins have special salt glands above their eyes that filter excess salt from their blood. This allows them to drink seawater and eat salty fish without getting dehydrated.

- **Gripping Feet:** Their bright orange webbed feet are great for paddling underwater, but they also have sharp claws for clinging to steep, rocky cliffs where they nest.

These incredible adaptations allow puffins to thrive in one of Earth's most challenging environments—the cold, stormy North Atlantic Ocean.

Fun Fact: Puffins can drink salt water because they have special glands near their eyes that filter out the salt.

Fun Fact: Puffin pairs often greet each other after fishing trips with a behavior called "billing" that looks like they are sword-fighting with their beaks.

What Do Puffins Eat?

Puffins are piscivores—fish specialists that have evolved amazing hunting skills to catch their slippery prey both above and below the water's surface. Their diet consists almost entirely of small fish, though they occasionally eat marine worms, crustaceans, and squid.

Their favorite foods include herring, sardines, anchovies, sand eels, and capelin—small, silvery fish that swim in large schools near the ocean surface. The exact species they eat depends on what's available in their local waters and the season.

Puffins are spectacular underwater hunters. They dive from the surface or plunge from the air, using their wings to propel themselves through the water at speeds up to 6 mph (10 km/h). Unlike penguins, which use only their feet for underwater swimming, puffins "fly" through the water using their wings, making them incredibly agile and fast.

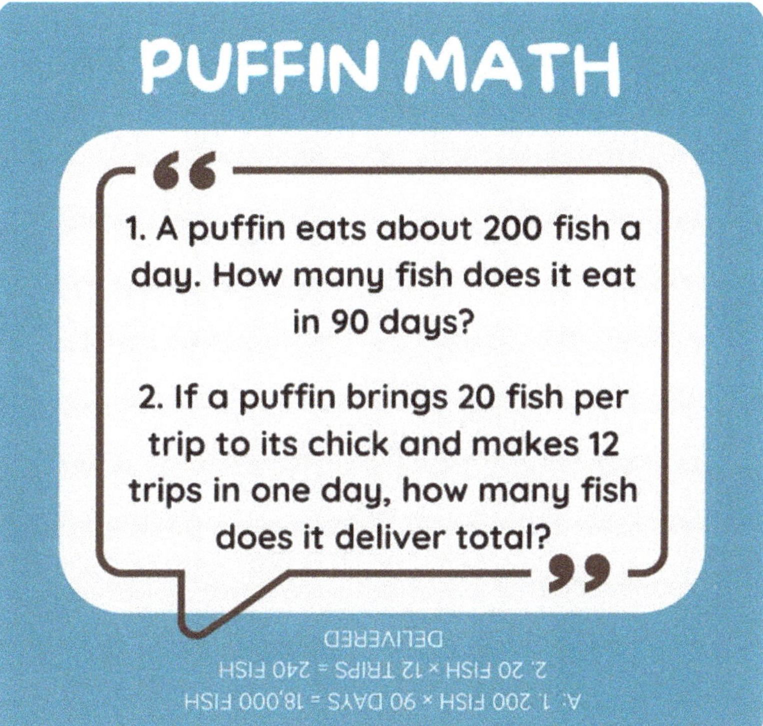

Once underwater, puffins can stay submerged for up to one minute while chasing schools of fish. Their excellent underwater vision helps them spot and target individual fish, even in murky water. They typically hunt at depths of 15 to 50 feet (5 to 15 meters), though they can dive much deeper when necessary.

What makes puffins truly special is their ability to catch multiple fish in a single dive. During breeding season, their beaks develop special adaptations—backward-pointing spines on the roof of their mouth and tongue—that allow them to hold fish crosswise while continuing to hunt. A single puffin can carry 10 to 30 small fish back to its chick, with the record being an incredible 62 fish in one trip!

When not feeding chicks, adult puffins often eat their catch immediately underwater. They need to consume large amounts of fish to maintain their energy for flying, diving, and staying warm in cold ocean waters. During the summer months, an adult puffin might catch and consume 100 to 300 small fish per day, especially when feeding a hungry chick.

Life in the Colony

For most of the year, puffins are solitary travelers, scattered across the vast North Atlantic Ocean. But when breeding season arrives in late spring, something incredible happens—thousands of puffins gather on coastal cliffs and islands, creating some of the most spectacular seabird gatherings in the world.

These breeding colonies, called puffinries, can range in size from just a few dozen pairs to hundreds of thousands of birds. The biggest colonies are found on remote islands where puffins have returned for generations. Arriving at a major puffin colony during peak season is like entering a bustling seabird city, filled with constant activity, noise, and color.

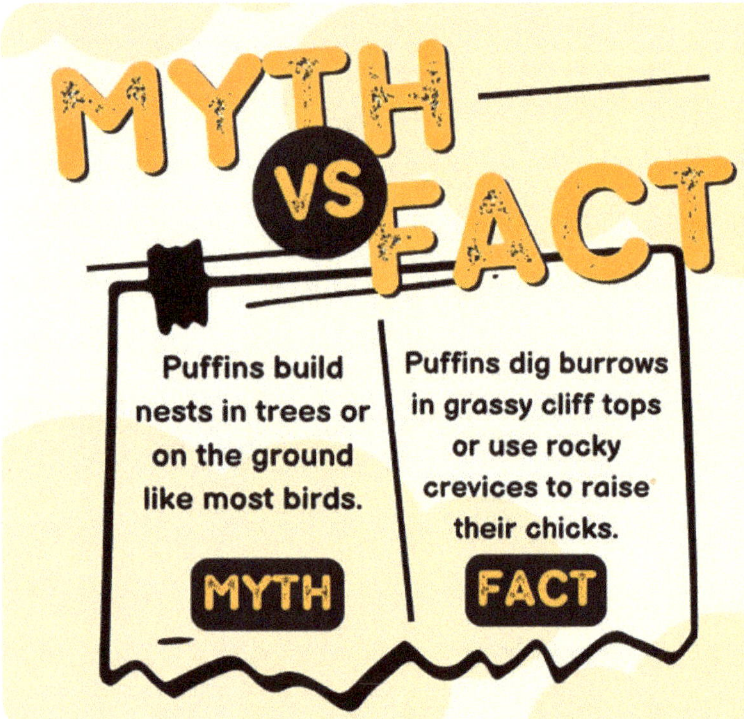

Puffins are surprisingly social during breeding season. They engage in elaborate courtship displays, including "billing"—touching and tapping their colorful beaks together in what looks like kissing. These displays help strengthen pair bonds and show off the health and fitness of potential mates.

Within the colony, puffins establish territories around their nesting burrows. While they're generally peaceful birds, they will defend their burrows from intruders through threatening displays, loud calls, and occasionally physical confrontations. Most disputes are settled through intimidation rather than actual fighting.

Young puffins, called pufflings, remain hidden in burrows for most of their early lives. However, adult puffins are constantly coming and going, bringing fish to their chicks and maintaining their burrows. The result is a colony that buzzes with activity from dawn to dusk throughout the breeding season.

After the breeding season ends in late summer, the colony quickly empties as puffins return to their solitary ocean lives. The dramatic transformation from a crowded, noisy community to an empty, silent cliff happens within just a few weeks.

Fun Fact: Puffins can flap their wings so fast they sometimes appear blurry, like hummingbirds.

On the Move

Puffins are among the most impressive long-distance travelers in the animal kingdom. These small seabirds spend eight to nine months of each year wandering across thousands of miles of open ocean, following fish and favorable weather.

Unlike many migratory birds that follow predictable routes, puffins have a more wandering lifestyle. After leaving their breeding colonies in late summer, they scatter across the North Atlantic. Some head south toward warmer waters, while others travel north toward Greenland and the Arctic. Individual puffins have been tracked more than 3,000 miles (4,800 km) from their breeding sites.

What makes puffin navigation so amazing is that they cross the ocean without any land-marks to guide them. Scientists believe puffins use a mix of Earth's magnetic fields, the sun, the stars, and even smell to find their way. Their internal compass is so accurate that they can return to the exact same burrow year after year.

These ocean journeys are not easy. Puffins must find rich feeding areas while avoiding storms, predators, and empty patches of sea. Climate change is making things harder, too, as warming waters push fish farther away.

Still, puffins return to their breeding colonies with amazing precision, often arriving with-in days of the same date each year. That perfect schedule helps them reunite with their mates and catch the peak season for fish near the colony.

A Day in the Life

A puffin's daily routine depends on where it is—either at sea or at the colony. While life on the ocean is simple and quiet, life at the colony is busy, noisy, and nonstop.

When puffins are out at sea—sometimes for eight months at a time—their days revolve around food and survival.

Before dawn, puffins begin scanning the water for fish. They may float calmly, watching below, or take flight to search for better feeding areas. Once they spot a school of fish, they dive fast, using their wings like flippers to chase prey underwater.

They make dozens of dives per day, swimming, catching fish, and resurfacing to rest. Between hunts, puffins bob on the ocean's surface, their waterproof feathers keeping them warm and dry—even in icy seas.

Puffins also spend time preening, using oil from a special gland to keep their feathers in top shape. Clean, waterproof feathers are essential for staying afloat and flying long distances.

During breeding season, everything changes. Each day begins with burrow duty. Puffins check their underground nests to make sure they're clean, dry, and safe from collapse. They may clear out dirt, line it with grass, or rebuild fallen walls.

Then it's time to fish for their chicks. Adults fly out to sea, dive for small fish, and return with their catch. Some puffins make a dozen or more trips per day to feed their puffling.

Between trips, puffins interact with neighbors, defend their territory, and spend time with their mate. You'll see pairs billing (beak tapping), resting together, or flying in loops over the colony.

As evening arrives, adults return to the burrow. They take turns caring for their chick, while their partner goes back out to fish. In the long daylight hours of the northern summer, activity may continue well into the night.

Fun Fact: Baby puffins are called pufflings, but a group of puffins on land is called a "circus" and a group floating on water is a "raft."

Fun Fact: Pufflings grow so fast they can double their weight in just one week.

Mating and Birth

When puffins arrive at their breeding colonies in late spring, they face one of their most important tasks—finding or reuniting with a mate. Puffins are generally monogamous, often returning to the same partner and same nesting site year after year.

The mating process begins after pairs reestablish their bond through courtship displays like beak-tapping ("billing") and synchronized flying. Once bonded, the real work begins: building a safe, dry home for their future chick.

Puffin nest construction is serious business. Using their sharp claws and powerful beaks, pairs work together to excavate burrows in the soft clifftop soil. These tunnels extend 2 to 3 feet (60 to 90 cm) underground, ending in a circular chamber lined with grass, feathers, and seaweed. Some pairs return to the same burrow year after year, expanding and improving their underground home.

Timing is everything. Female puffins lay a single large, white egg only when local fish populations are at their peak. This ensures that when the chick hatches six weeks later, there will be plenty of food nearby.

The egg itself is quite large—it weighs about 15% of the female's body weight. Both parents share incubation duties, taking turns warming the egg with special bare patches of skin on their bellies called brood patches. They switch roles every few hours, with one parent always staying with the egg while the other goes fishing.

Over the 42-day incubation period, the parents must protect the egg from temperature changes, predators, and disturbance. The egg is rarely left alone, and it's kept at a steady 99°F (37°C) for proper development.

When hatching time comes, the parents can hear tiny peeps coming from inside the shell. Sometimes they help by rotating the egg, but usually the strong little puffling hatches on its own, using a temporary egg tooth—a sharp bump on its beak that falls off shortly after birth.

Growing Up Puffin

Baby puffins, called pufflings, begin life as tiny, helpless chicks covered in soft gray down. At hatching, they weigh just 1.5 ounces (42 grams), about the same as a golf ball. Even though they are small, pufflings mean a lot of hard work for their parents, who will spend the next six to eight weeks raising their single chick.

Life for a puffling takes place entirely underground. Hidden deep in the burrow, the chick is safe from dangers above, like gulls, skuas, and ravens that patrol the colony looking for easy prey. The burrow keeps pufflings warm, safe, and out of sight while they grow.

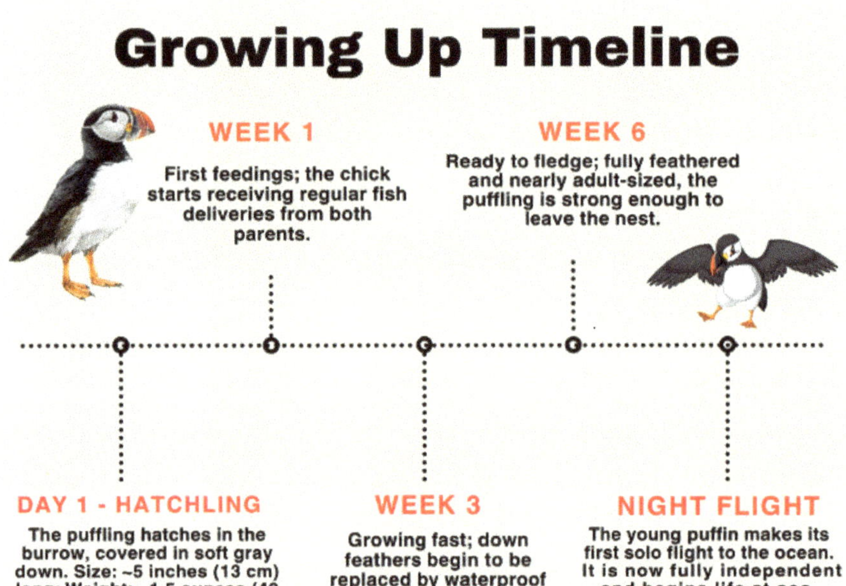

Puffling parents are incredibly dedicated. Both adults make multiple fishing trips every day, sometimes flying many miles to find the best fishing spots. When they return, their beaks are packed with small fish arranged crosswise, a spectacular sight that looks like a colorful, living mustache.

Parents don't just drop off food and leave. They spend time in the burrow with their chick, keeping it warm, grooming, and bonding. Pufflings quickly learn to recognize their parents' calls and respond with excited begging sounds when they hear familiar voices coming through the tunnel.

Inside the burrow, pufflings grow fast, building up their flight muscles and developing waterproof feathers. Young puffins have small, dark beaks and lack the bright orange colors they will grow as adults.

The most dramatic moment in a puffling's life is fledging, its very first journey from burrow to ocean. This usually happens at night, when predators are less active. There is no training and no practice. The puffling must head to sea and take off on its own, relying only on instinct. Those that reach the water immediately begin their independent ocean lives, learning to fish, dive, and survive entirely on their own.

Fun Fact: Puffins have small claws on their webbed feet that help them grip steep cliffs and dig burrows.

Fun Fact: A puffin's heart can beat up to 400 times per minute during flight to keep up with its fast-flapping wings.

Puffins and Their Ecosystem

Puffins are more than charismatic seabirds. They are important players in both ocean and coastal ecosystems, connecting land and sea in ways that support many other plants and animals.

Marine Food Web: Puffins are expert fish hunters. By feeding on species like herring, sardines, and sand eels, they help keep fish populations in balance. A single colony of 10,000 puffin pairs can eat more than 100 tons of fish during one breeding season!

Nutrient Movers: Puffins bring nutrients from the sea to the land. The fish they eat are digested and released as guano (bird droppings), which fertilizes the soil around puffin colonies. This helps unique plants and grasses grow in places that would otherwise be bare.

Indicator Species: Scientists study puffin populations to learn about ocean health. Changes in puffin survival, chick growth, or nesting success often signal shifts in fish populations, rising sea temperatures, or pollution. When puffins struggle, it is often a warning sign for the whole ecosystem.

Habitat Creation: Puffin burrows do more than shelter chicks. Once abandoned, they become homes for rabbits, storm petrels, and other creatures. The digging also loosens the soil, helping rare plants and insects survive on cliff tops.

Seed Spreaders: While puffins mainly eat fish, they sometimes snack on berries and seeds near their nests. As they move around the colony, they help spread seeds and give plants a chance to grow in new places.

Tourism and Education: Puffins attract millions of visitors each year to cliffs and islands across the North Atlantic. Their charm supports local economies and inspires people to protect seabirds and their habitats.

Healthy puffin colonies are a sign of thriving oceans with plenty of fish, clean water, and stable coastlines. Protecting puffins helps protect the whole ocean world they depend on.

Natural Predators

Adult puffins are fast, agile, and spend most of the year far out at sea. Still, they face real dangers, especially at the colony during breeding season.

Gulls: Great black-backed gulls and herring gulls are the most common puffin predators. They use their size to overpower adults or steal the fish puffins are carrying.

Skuas: These powerful seabirds use aerial ambushes to force puffins to drop their catch. Sometimes they attack and kill adult puffins outright.

Ravens and Crows: These smart birds patrol colonies searching for unguarded eggs or young pufflings.

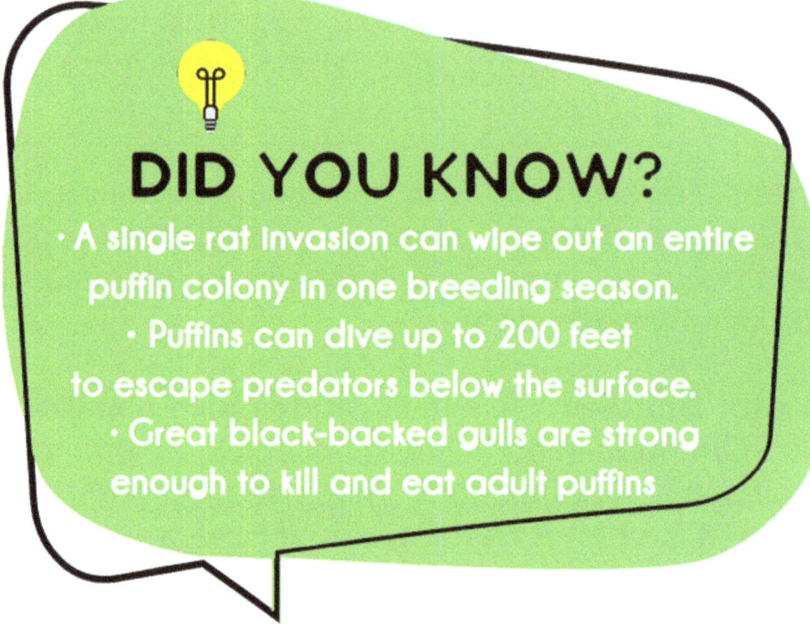

Ground Predators: Foxes, rats, and weasels can cause terrible losses if they reach a nesting island. That's why puffins usually breed only on remote islands without land-based predators.

Ocean Hunters: Large fish like cod and halibut, and sometimes sharks and seals, may catch puffins underwater.

Defense Strategies

Puffins have several ways to stay safe:

- Fast escape dives and quick takeoffs
- Underground burrows that shield chicks from nearly all predators
- Colony living, with thousands of eyes watching for danger
- Fishing during early morning or evening when gulls and skuas are less active

Living in a dangerous world, puffins have evolved clever strategies that help keep both adults and chicks safe.

Fun Fact: Puffins can sleep while floating on the ocean, bobbing on the waves like tiny feathered boats.

Fun Fact: A puffin's orange feet turn a brighter shade during breeding season, helping them show off to potential mates.

Challenges and Threats

Puffins have survived for thousands of years in the harsh North Atlantic, but today they face new challenges, many caused by humans and climate change.

Climate Change: As oceans warm, the small fish puffins rely on are moving farther north. Puffins must travel longer distances to find food, leaving their chicks hungry.

Ocean Pollution: Puffins often swallow plastic debris, mistaking it for food. Oil spills are especially dangerous because oil ruins the waterproofing on their feathers, which can lead to drowning or hypothermia.

Overfishing: Large fishing boats compete with puffins for the same small fish. When fish populations drop, puffins struggle to feed their chicks.

Light Pollution: Pufflings leave their burrows at night and follow moonlight on the ocean to find the sea. Bright town lights confuse them, and many end up stranded far from water.

Tourism: Boats and visitors that come too close can frighten puffins away from their burrows.

Despite these threats, puffins still have a chance. Conservation efforts are making a difference through protected habitats, light-reduction programs, fishing rules, and public education.

- **Reduce plastic use** – Puffins often mistake plastic for food. Use reusable bags, bottles, and containers to help keep oceans clean.
- **Keep beaches clean** – Pick up trash during beach walks or join a local cleanup to protect seabirds and marine life.
- **Support sustainable seafood** – Ask adults to choose fish caught using eco-friendly methods that don't compete with puffins for food.
- **Stay on trails when visiting nesting areas** – Don't disturb burrows or get too close to puffins and their chicks.
- **Learn and share** – Read books, watch documentaries, and tell others about puffins. Awareness is the first step toward action!

Life Span and Population

In the wild, puffins typically live 15 to 20 years, though some reach their late twenties. The oldest known wild puffin was at least 36 years old when last seen, which is impressive considering how much energy puffins spend flying, diving, and raising chicks.

Scientists use leg bands and small tracking devices to follow individual birds from year to year.

Global Numbers: Today, about 12 to 14 million puffins live worldwide, most of them Atlantic puffins.

Iceland: Home to about 60 percent of the world's Atlantic puffins, with 3 to 4 million breeding pairs. It's the puffin capital of the world.

Europe: Norway, the Faroe Islands, Scotland, and Ireland all host large populations.

North America: Populations are much smaller but show signs of hope. At Eastern Egg Rock in Maine, where puffins disappeared nearly a century ago, more than 150 breeding pairs now nest thanks to successful restoration efforts.

Declining Colonies: In Iceland and the Faroe Islands, some colonies have shrunk by more than 70 percent since the 1980s, mostly because of climate change.

Stable Colonies: Some Scottish and Norwegian colonies have stayed stable or even grown slightly in recent years.

Scientists consider puffins vulnerable to future threats. Careful monitoring and continued conservation work will help make sure puffins keep thriving for generations to come.

Fun Fact: Iceland alone has so many puffins that they out-number the country's human population by about ten to one.

Conclusion

Throughout this book, we have seen that puffins are far more amazing than their clownish appearance suggests. From their underwater "flight" to their epic ocean journeys, puffins are perfectly built for one of the toughest environments on Earth.

Puffins teach us lessons about teamwork, loyalty, and connection. Their lifelong pair bonds and devoted parenting show how wildlife has adapted in extraordinary ways over millions of years.

They are also important signs of ocean health. When puffin colonies struggle, it often means bigger problems in the ocean, problems that affect fish, other seabirds, and even people.

Today, puffins face serious threats: climate change, pollution, overfishing, and habitat disturbance. But their story is also one of hope. The return of puffins to Maine shows what is possible when communities, scientists, and governments work together to protect wildlife.

Each of us can help. By reducing plastic use, supporting sustainable fishing, or simply spreading awareness, we can make a difference for puffins and the oceans they call home.

The story of the puffin is really a story of connection, between people and the planet, between action and impact. With understanding and care, we can give these wonderful seabirds a bright future.

Test Your Puffin Knowledge!

Think you remember everything about these colorful seabirds? See how many questions you can answer!

1. What is the scientific name of the Atlantic puffin?
A) Fratercula arctica B) Puffinus puffinus C) Alca torda D) Pinguinus impennis

2. True or False: Puffins use their wings to "fly" underwater.

3. How many small fish has a record-holding puffin been seen carrying in its beak at once?
A) 12 B) 30 C) 62 D) 100

4. What are baby puffins called?
A) Chicks B) Pufflings C) Puffkins D) Hatchlings

5. Which country is home to about 60 percent of the world's Atlantic puffin population?
A) Norway B) Iceland C) Canada D) Scotland

6. How deep can an Atlantic puffin dive?
A) 20 feet (6 m) B) 50 feet (15 m) C) 200 feet (60 m) D) 500 feet (152 m)

7. What is a puffin nesting area called?
A) A herd B) A pod C) A colony D) A pack

8. How do puffins find their way across the open ocean?
A) Magnetic fields and sun position B) GPS C) Following other birds D) Only by smell

9. Which of these is NOT one of the three puffin species?
A) Atlantic puffin B) Horned puffin C) Tufted puffin D) Arctic puffin

10. What famous nickname do puffins have because of their colorful beaks?
A) Sea eagles B) Clowns of the sea C) Ocean kings D) Rainbow divers

Answer Key: 1-A, 2-True, 3-C, 4-B, 5-B, 6-C, 7-C, 8-A, 9-D, 10-B

STEM Challenge: Think Like a Scientist!

Puffins have incredible adaptations that help them survive in the cold North Atlantic. Try these fun, hands-on science experiments to discover how their bodies help them thrive on sea and land!

Waterproof Feather Experiment

Topic: Adaptation & Water Resistance

You'll Need:
2 feathers (craft store) or 2 paper towels, cooking oil, water in a spray bottle, two small plates.

What to Do:
1. Coat one feather or paper towel with a light layer of cooking oil and leave the other untouched.
2. Place both on plates.
3. Spray each with water and watch what happens.

Which one stays drier?

What You'll Learn:
Puffins spread natural oil from a special gland all over their feathers while preening. This oil forms a waterproof coating that lets water roll right off, keeping them warm and dry even in icy ocean water.

Fish-Carrying Beak Challenge

Topic: Biology & Engineering

You'll Need:
A spring-loaded clothespin, 10 small rubber bands or paper strips, a timer.

What to Do:
1. Open the clothespin and see how many rubber bands you can hold across the jaws at once without dropping any.
2. Try adding one at a time, carrying them 10 steps, and placing them in a bowl (your "burrow").
3. Time yourself. How many "fish" can you carry in one trip?
4. Try again, but this time hold them all sideways (crosswise) like a puffin does.

What You'll Learn:
Puffins have backward-pointing spines on the roof of their mouth and tongue that hold fish in place while they keep hunting. Holding prey crosswise means they can fit many more fish than they could by carrying them tip-first, just like you carried more rubber bands when you lined them up neatly.

Word Search

```
O S V A T F L X E D S A M I O
N G X N Q X L I S G I K N K A
W Y Q M T R U E N A X O A Y W
W O R R U B P I D N A E C O N
N A G W N A W K L G B U H U Z
B C H I C K S Q N X E C Y C C
S G U S M I G R A T I O N I Z
D E P C L I B A I C O H T T K
N I A N E G A M U L P N F C Y
H E V B W D S Y K Z A F I R R
N K S E I H H N X L J E S A O
I T Q T O R Y G T O B A H N T
F V Z W G N D A D Q I T X N I
F O I Q O Q W S K C L H O D R
U P U L S W U Q F L L E E F R
P N O E R Q Y K Q I I R Q A E
U C B F E R Q Z J F N S D W T
P X I C E L A N D F G W R C U
```

Arctic	Colony	Nest
Atlantic	Dive	Ocean
Beak	Feathers	Plumage
Billing	Fish	Puffin
Burrow	Fledge	Seabirds
Chick	Iceland	Territory
Cliff	Migration	Wings

Glossary

adaptations – special features or behaviors that help a plant or animal survive in its home

Alcidae – the family of seabirds that includes puffins, auks, murres, and guillemots

billing – a puffin courtship behavior in which pairs tap and rub their beaks together

brood patches – bare patches of skin on a parent bird's belly used to warm an egg

burrow – an underground tunnel or hole that an animal digs as a home

colony – a large group of seabirds that gather to nest in the same area

ecosystem – all the living things and their environment in an area

fledging – the moment a young bird leaves the nest for the first time

guano – bird droppings that fertilize the soil

incubation – the process of keeping an egg warm until it hatches

migratory – moving from one place to another, usually with the seasons

monogamous – having only one mate for a long period of time, often for life

piscivores – animals that eat mainly fish

plumage – all the feathers that cover a bird's body

predators – animals that hunt other animals for food

preening – the way birds clean, arrange, and waterproof their feathers with their beaks

puffling – a baby puffin

puffinry – a breeding colony of puffins

Resources and References

Want to learn more about puffins and the North Atlantic? Check out these trusted books, websites, and organizations that explore wildlife, science, and conservation across the sea and sky.

Books

Project Puffin: How We Brought Puffins Back to Egg Rock by Stephen W. Kress and Pete Salmansohn (Tilbury House) — The true story of how puffins returned to the coast of Maine.

Puffins by Gail Gibbons (Holiday House) — A colorful, kid-friendly introduction to puffin life, with simple facts and bright illustrations.

Nights of the Pufflings by Bruce McMillan (Houghton Mifflin) — Follow the kids of Heimaey Island, Iceland, as they rescue baby puffins lost in the dark.

Websites

National Geographic Kids – Atlantic Puffin
kids.nationalgeographic.com/animals/birds/facts/atlantic-puffin
Fun facts, videos, and photos about puffins and their ocean home.

Audubon Project Puffin
projectpuffin.audubon.org
Learn how scientists helped puffins return to Maine and how you can help protect them.

RSPB – Puffin Facts for Kids
rspb.org.uk/fun-and-learning/fun-for-kids/facts-about-nature/facts-about-birds/puffin
Puffin facts, activities, and videos from the Royal Society for the Protection of Birds.

For Young Scientists

Seabird Watch
seabirdwatch.org
Help real scientists count puffins by looking at photos from seabird colonies.

Explore.org – Puffin Cam
explore.org/livecams/puffins
Watch live webcams from puffin colonies during breeding season.

National Audubon Society – Atlantic Puffin
audubon.org/field-guide/bird/atlantic-puffin
A trusted guide to puffin biology, habitat, and conservation.

Keep Exploring!

If you enjoyed learning about sea otters, explore other titles in the This Incredible Planet series to discover more amazing animals—from sea turtles to penguins to elephants—and the habitats they call home.

Index